Rebecca Hunter with Angela Davies

In Grandma's Day
Christmas In Grandma's Day
Grandma's War
Having Fun In Grandma's Day
Home Life In Grandma's Day
School Life In Grandma's Day
Shopping In Grandma's Day
Travelling In Grandma's Day

Published by Evans Brothers Ltd
2A Portman Mansions
Chiltern Street
London W1M 1LE
England

First published in 1999
First published in paperback in 1999
Printed in Hong Kong

British Library Cataloguing in Publication Data
Hunter, Rebecca
Shopping: in Grandma's Day. - (In Grandma's Day)
1. Shopping - Great Britain - History - 20th century - Juvenile literature
I. Title
381.1'0904

ISBN 0 237 52006 0

Acknowledgements
Planning and production by Discovery Books
Edited by Rebecca Hunter
Designed by Ian Winton
Illustrations by Stuart Lafford

The publishers would like to thank Angela Davies and Kathleen Wood for their help in the preparation of this book, and The Collector's Gallery, Shrewsbury for the loan of the notes and coins on pages 12 and 13.

For permission to reproduce copyright material, the author and publishers gratefully acknowledge the following:
The Advertising Archives 15 (middle), 18 (right); 19 The Hulton Getty Picture Collection Library 9, 10, 11, 14, 18 (left), 21, 22, 23, 25 (bottom), 27 (bottom), 28 (top), cover (right); The Robert Opie Collection 8 (top), 15, 17 (top, bottom); Derek Foxton 18, 19, 24, 26, cover (left); The Frith Collection 20; The Gloucester Collection 27 (top).

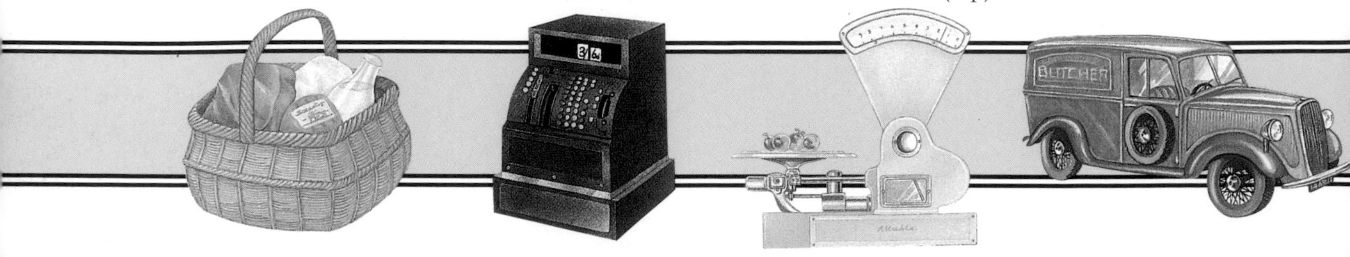

CONTENTS

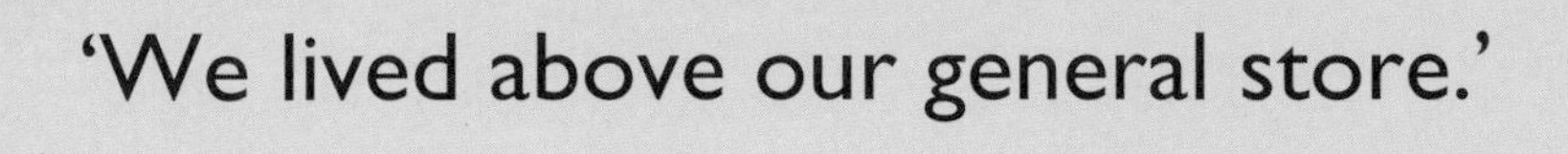

'We lived above our general store.'

My name is Angela and I am a grandmother. I have three grandchildren. This photo shows me with Alice who is eleven and Fergus who is ten.

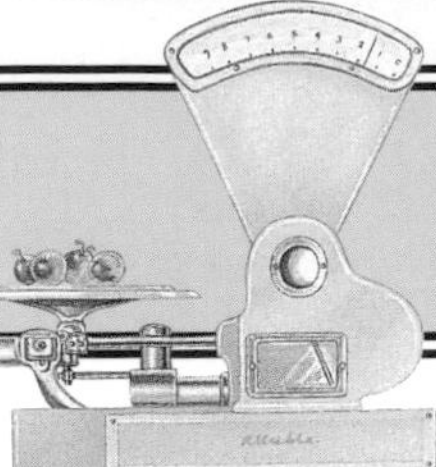

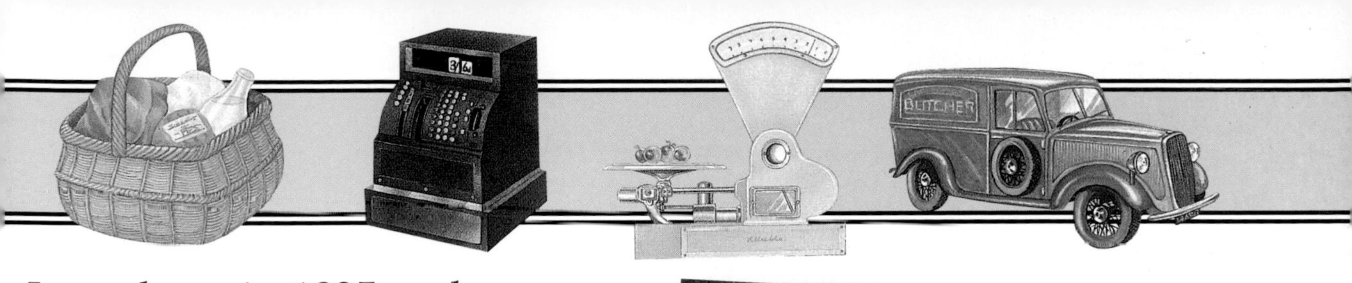

I was born in 1935 and grew up in a village called Burley Gate in Herefordshire. We lived above a post office and general store owned by my parents. My father was a coach driver and my mum ran the post office and shop.

Shops were very different in those days and I am going to tell you what shopping was like then.

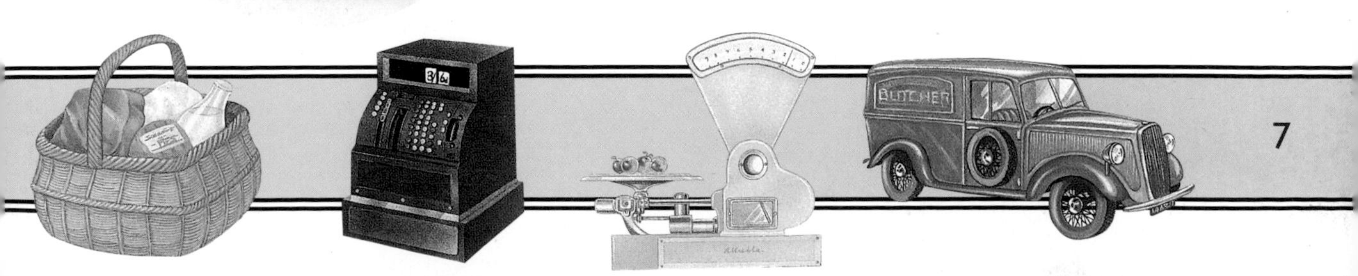

'People queued at the counter.'

Our shop stood on a corner at the centre of the village. It was a red brick building with a white picket fence around it. There was a little bell on the door that rang when anyone came in. Inside there were shelves from floor to ceiling filled with packets, bottles, jars and tins.

Burley Gate Post Office and Police Station.

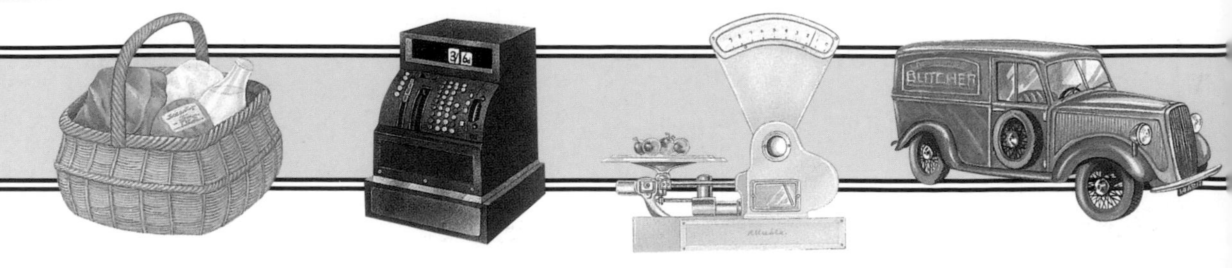

There was no self-service in those days and no carrier bags either. People brought their own bags or baskets with them. They waited in a queue at the **grocery** counter until it was their turn to be served. Then they told you what they wanted and you went and fetched it for them.

On one side of the shop was a marble-topped table where we sliced and weighed huge blocks of butter and whole cheeses.

'The bread was still warm.'

Villages today usually have just one shop, or sometimes no shops at all. When I was a girl, the bigger villages had lots of shops.

The village baker baked his own bread on the premises. Some people had it delivered to their homes by bicycle.

It was often still warm when it arrived at our house!

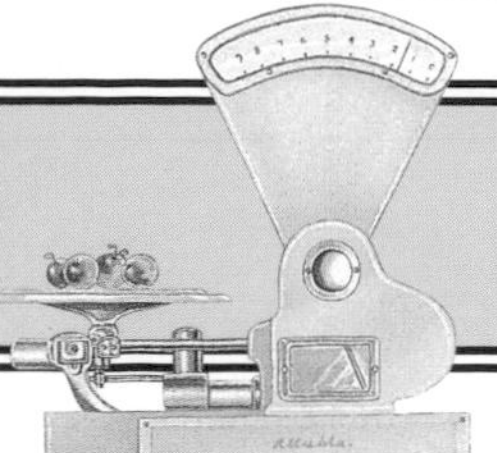

Butchers wore stripy aprons and laid out their produce on marble slabs in the window. Salted and fresh meat hung on hooks, often outside the shop.

The village greengrocer had all his fruit and vegetables set up outside the shop. He would tip your vegetables straight into your basket.

No one had refrigerators to keep food fresh in those days, so shopping had to be done every day.

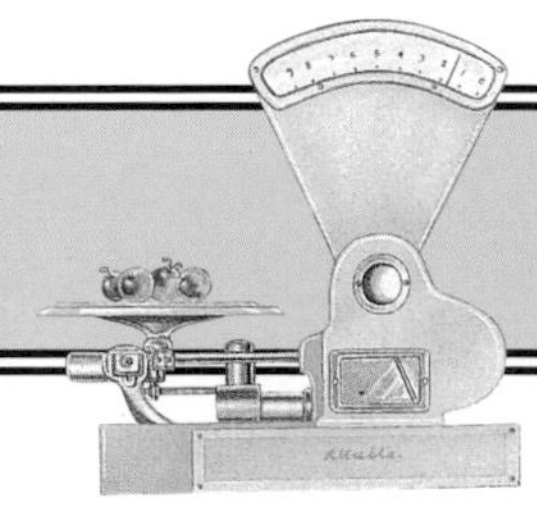

'We had pounds, shillings and pence.'

Money was different in those days. Instead of pounds and pence like today, we had pounds, **shillings** and pence. There were twelve pence (12d) to the shilling, and twenty shillings (20/-) to the pound (£1). A ha'penny was half a penny and a farthing was half a ha'penny. A two-shilling coin was called a florin and two shillings and sixpence (2/6) was half a crown.

We had many more types of coins and bank notes. You could get a one pound note and a ten shilling note. This would be like having a 50p note nowadays!

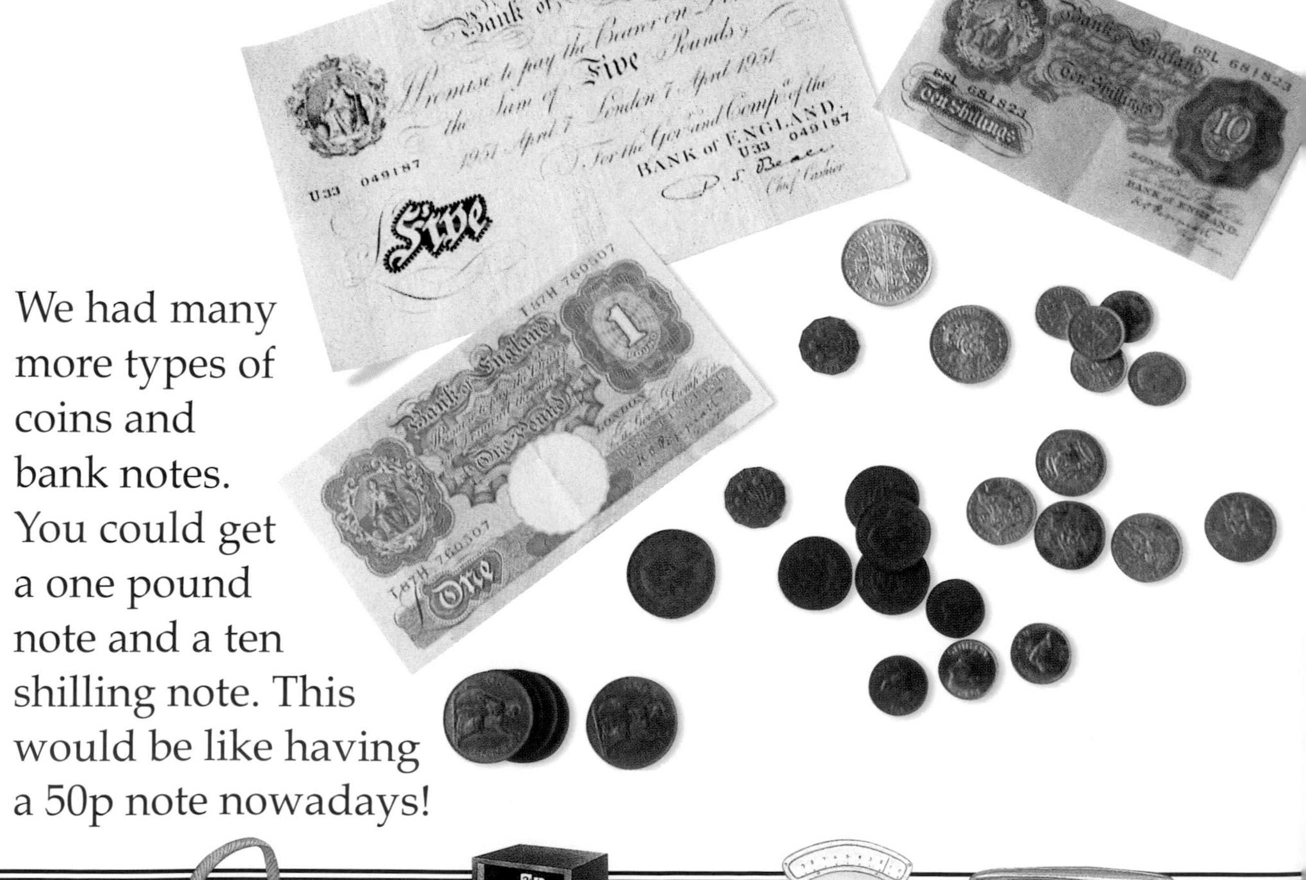

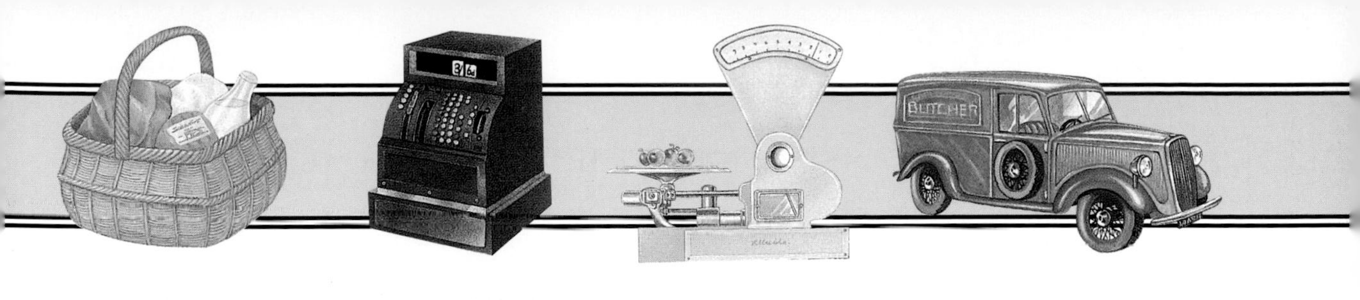

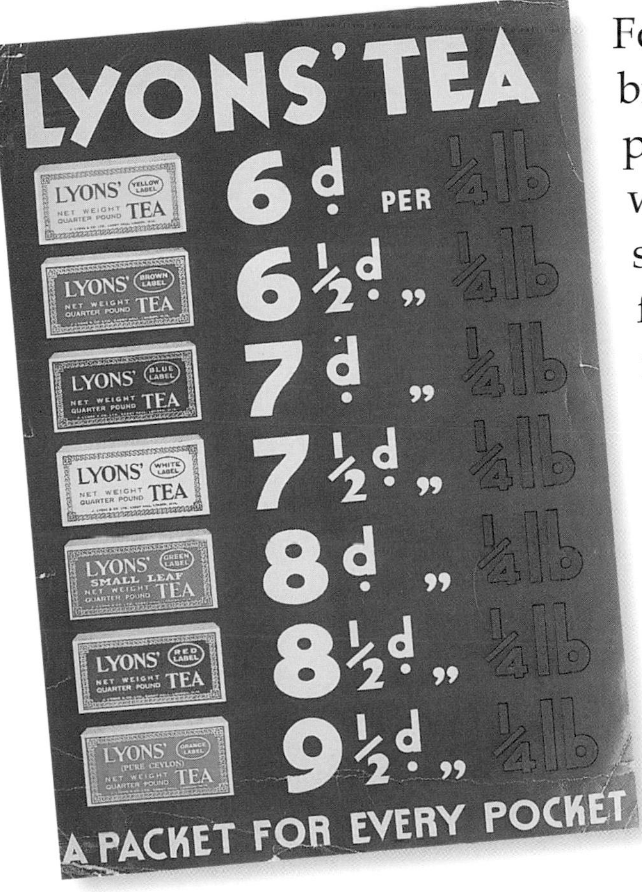

Food cost a lot less. A loaf of bread would cost about four pence ha'penny ($4\frac{1}{2}$d) which is worth about 2p today, and a small bun would be a penny farthing ($1\frac{1}{4}$d), less than 1p now!

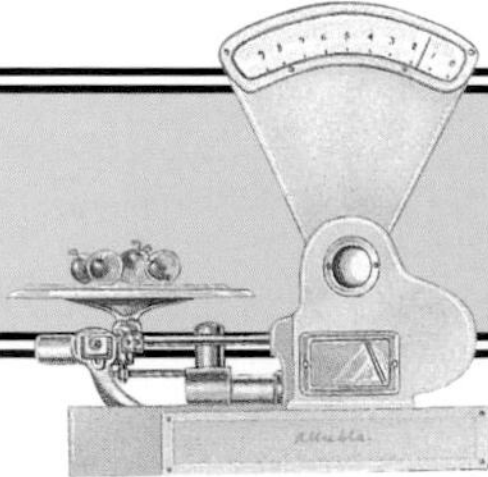

‘Food was not wrapped in plastic.’

I helped in the shop in the evenings and at weekends. Food in those days was not wrapped in plastic and packaged in cardboard; everything had to be weighed out separately. Things were weighed in **pounds** (lbs) and **ounces** (oz) then, not kilograms and grams like today.

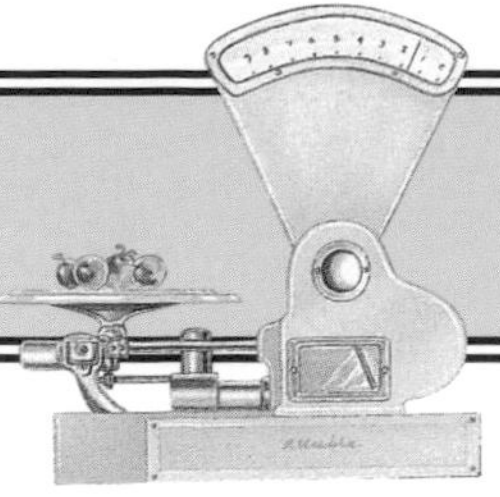

Biscuits were sold loose from 7lb tins. Flour and sugar arrived in large cloth sacks which stood on the floor. Using a small metal scoop, I would weigh out the amount required and put it in coloured paper bags: white for flour and blue for sugar.

I particularly enjoyed serving sweets to my friends. The most popular were Sherbert Fountains, which cost a ha'penny. Mars bars were more expensive and cost threepence ha'penny.

'Shopping took much longer.'

Sometimes we would go shopping in Hereford, our local town.

Shopping in town was very different then. There were many small shops and few big stores. Shopping took much longer because lots of different shops had to be visited.

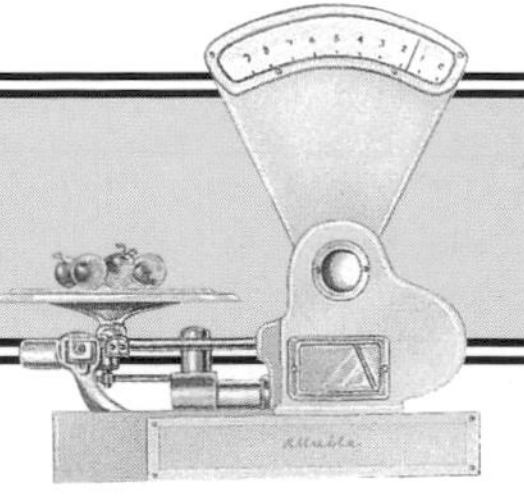

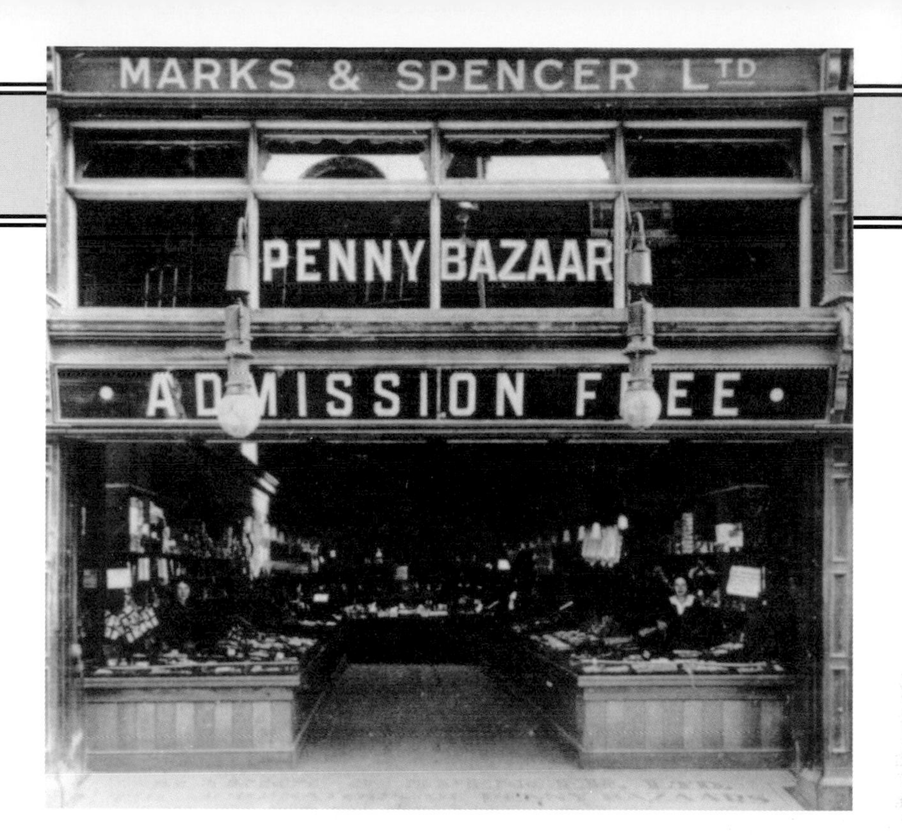

Many of today's large **chain stores** such as Woolworth's, Boots and Marks and Spencer existed but they were tiny compared to now and sold far fewer things.

Hereford also had a W H Smith and my mum belonged to their private library. While she was choosing her books, I would look at the comics, deciding which one to buy with my pocket money. I usually got *Chick's Own* or *Sunny Stories*.

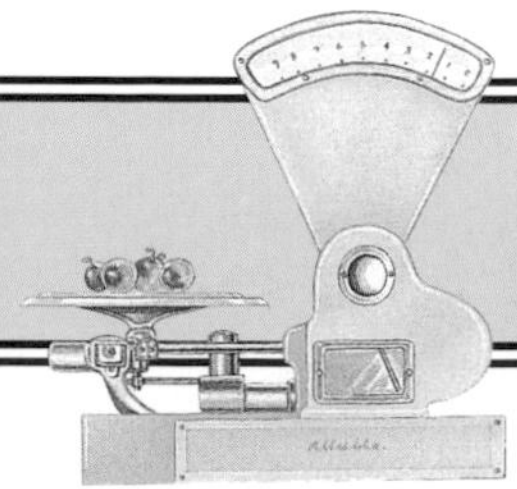

'Many people made their own clothes.'

In those days there were fewer clothing shops than there are today and clothes were expensive. So many people bought material and paper patterns to make their own clothes at home.

Occasionally we went into town to buy material for my clothes. At the **drapers** my mum would choose a pattern and I was allowed to choose the material.

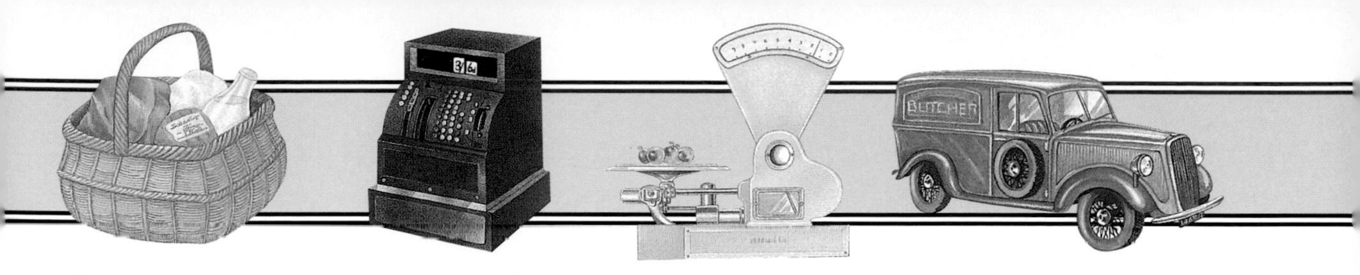

We also bought shoes in town. There weren't so many to choose from then. Some shoe shops had machines called pedoscopes which took x-rays of your feet to see how well your shoes fitted. A few years later doctors realised x-rays could damage your bones if used too often and so pedoscopes were banned.

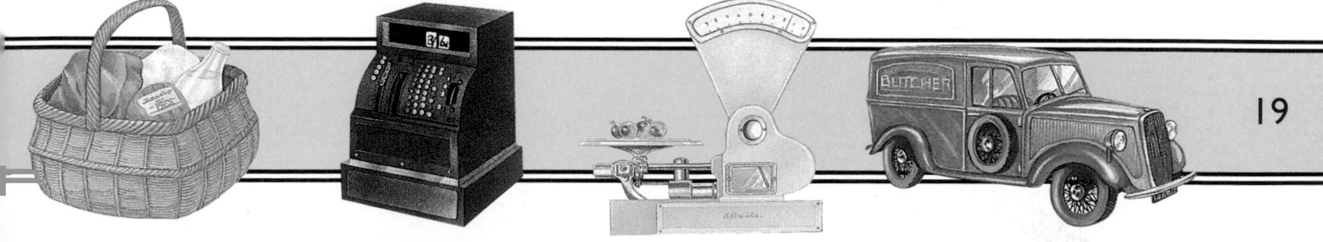

‘Market day in Hereford.’

Wednesday was market day in Hereford. All the farmers brought their **livestock** and **produce** to the market on this day. My mum closed the shop in the afternoon, so that she could go to the market. During the school holidays, I looked forward to Wednesdays, when I could go to the market too.

I enjoyed wandering among the pens in the livestock market, hearing the farmers haggle over the price of a pair of pigs or a flock of sheep.

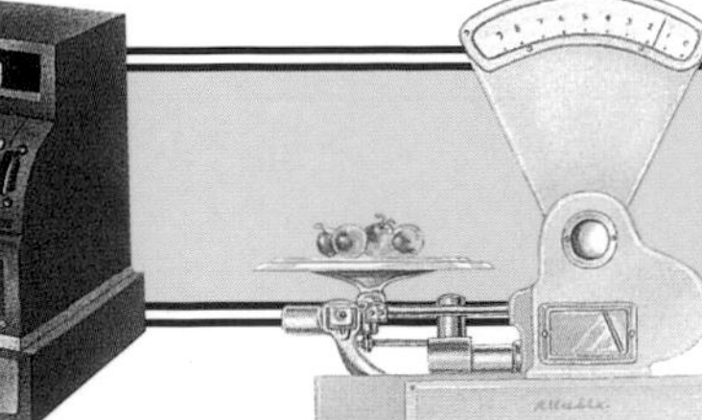

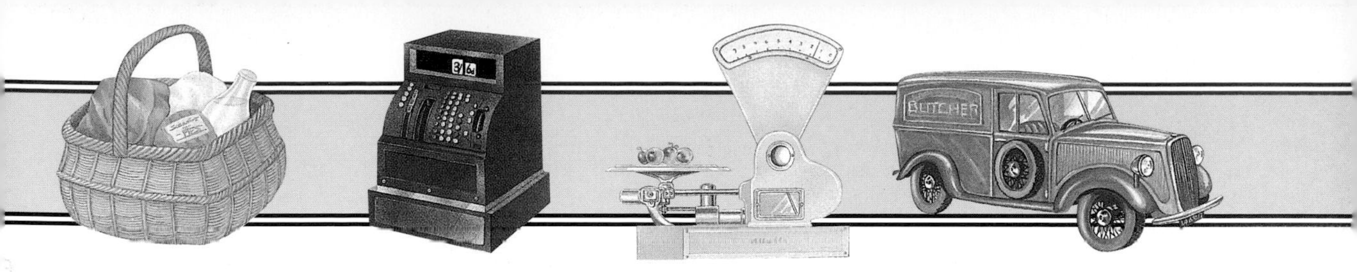

My mum was not interested in the animals. She wanted to wander round the market square looking at all the brightly coloured stalls. She enjoyed looking at the clothing stalls and bought fresh fruit and vegetables from the farmers' wives.

'Everybody had a ration book.'

During and after the Second World War, food was **rationed**. Everybody had a ration book with **coupons** which showed how much of each type of food they were allowed per week. Bacon, butter, cheese, sugar and sweets were some of the rationed foods that our shop sold. These had to be carefully measured out.

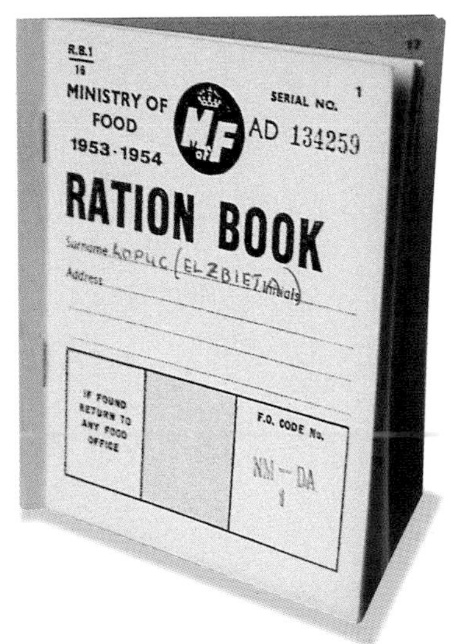

Children under five years old had green ration books. I thought it was very unfair when bananas arrived in the shops and were only available to green ration book customers!

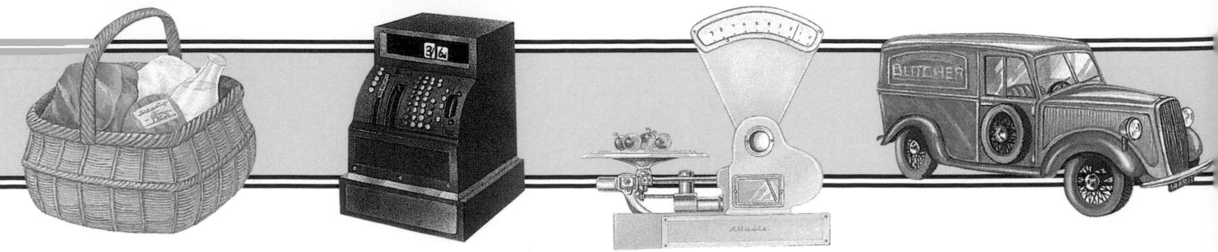

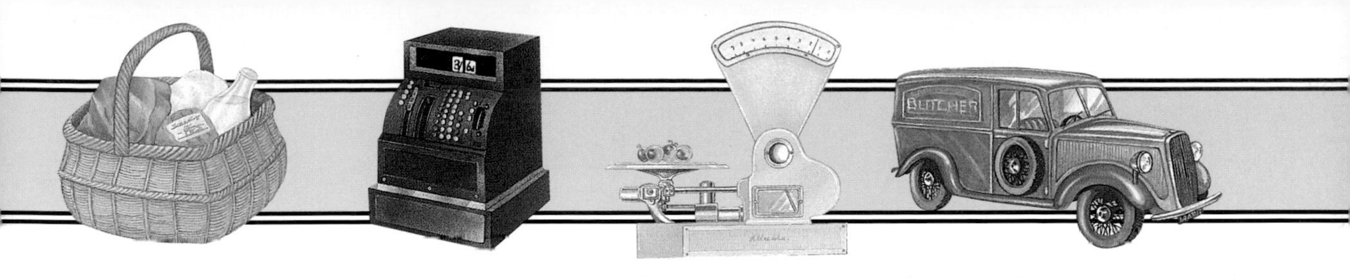

Every Saturday evening we had to count up the ration coupons we had received that week. My mum could only buy more stock for the shop with the coupons she had been given by the customers, so we were very careful not to lose any.

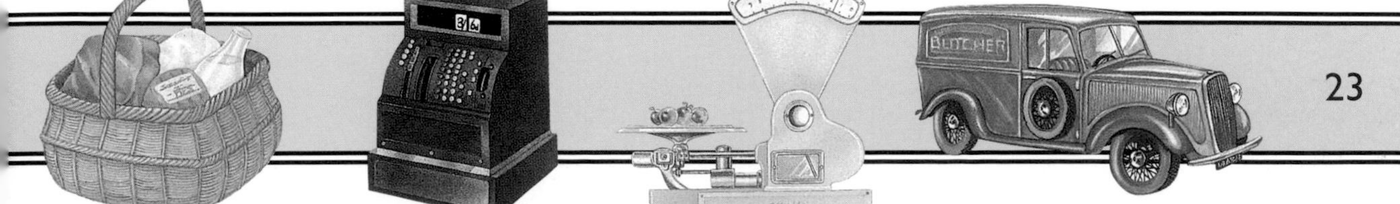

‘Mum had a mobile shop.’

Many shops had delivery vans so they could deliver goods to people who lived in the smaller **hamlets**. Here is a baker’s van from Hereford delivering bread to a remote farmhouse.

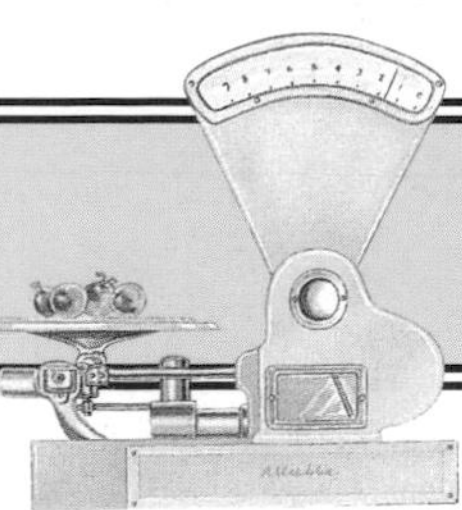

My mum had an old ambulance that had been made into a mobile shop. She used it in September to deliver food to the hop-pickers. Hundreds of people came down from Birmingham to help pick the hops. Whole families would live in a barn on the farm, sleeping on the hay and cooking on camp fires. My mum would sell them food and supplies from her mobile shop in the evenings.

Sometimes I was allowed to go and help with the hop-picking. We got paid by the **bushel**. I used the money I earned to save up for a bicycle that cost £10.

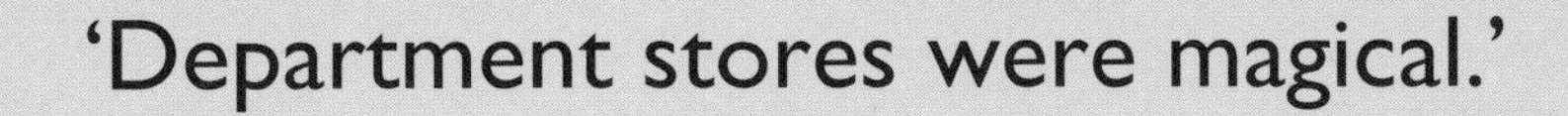

'Department stores were magical.'

As a Christmas treat we would go shopping in Gloucester. This was an exciting journey as we had to go by train. There were far more shops in Gloucester and they were much bigger than those in Hereford, with a better selection of goods.

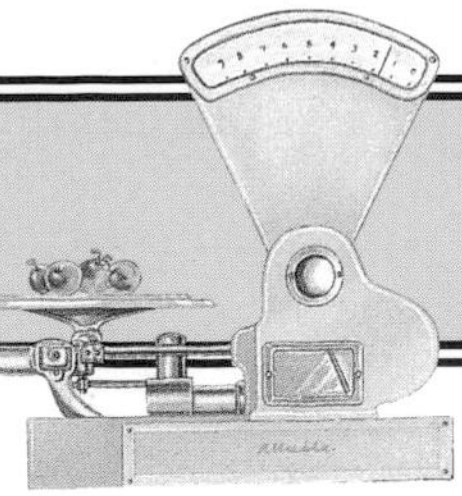

My favourite was the **department store** Bon Marche. I loved to travel in the lift, although my mum was always worried I would get my fingers caught in the metal doors!

At each floor the lift attendant would call out the floor number and what was sold on that floor. 'First floor **haberdashery** and shoes - going up.'

Department stores were magical places to me, I had never seen so many wonderful things as in the toy department at Christmas time!

'Shopping began to change.'

In the 1950s the first self-service supermarkets were introduced and shopping began to change.

Today supermarkets and shopping centres are so large that they have to be built on the edges of towns.

Many small village shops have closed since I was a child, but I am glad to say that our shop is still running as a post office. Here is a picture of it as it looks today with its present owner Mrs Hughes.

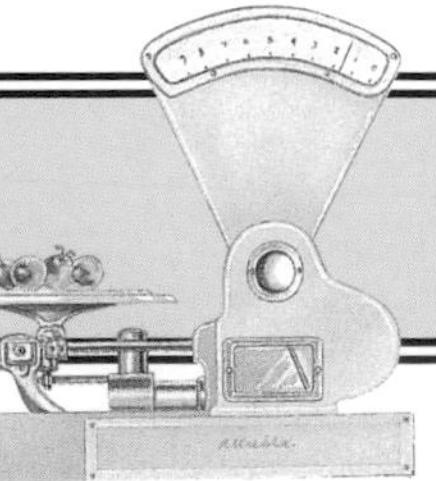

GLOSSARY

Bushel A measurement of volume for corn or fruit.
Chain stores A series of shops owned by the same company.
Coupons Detachable tickets allowing you to buy a certain amount of food or clothing.
Department store A large shop with many different departments.
Drapers A shop selling clothing fabric.
Groceries Foods and general household goods.
Haberdashery Small items of clothing and fabric.
Hamlet A group of houses: smaller than a village.
Livestock Animals kept by farmers.
Ounces A unit of weight: 1 ounce = 28 grams
Pounds (lbs) A unit of weight: 1lb = 0.45 kilogram.
Produce Fruit and vegetables grown for sale.
Rationing Limiting the amount of food and clothing that a person is allowed to buy.
Shilling A coin worth twelve old pence.

OTHER BOOKS TO READ

Other books about twentieth-century history for younger readers published by Evans include:

Rainbows *When Grandma Was Young*
Rainbows *When Dad Was Young*
Rainbows *What Was It Like Before Television?*
Tell Me About *Emmeline Pankhurst*
Tell Me About *Enid Blyton*
Britain Through The Ages *Britain Since 1930*
Alpha *1960s*
Take Ten Years *1930s, 1940s, 1950s, 1960s, 1970s, 1980s*

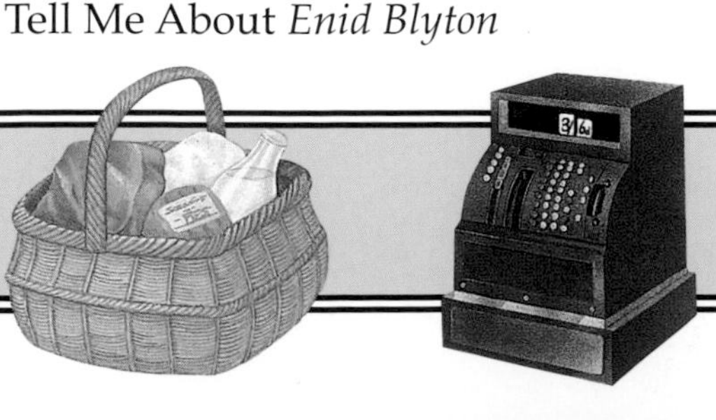

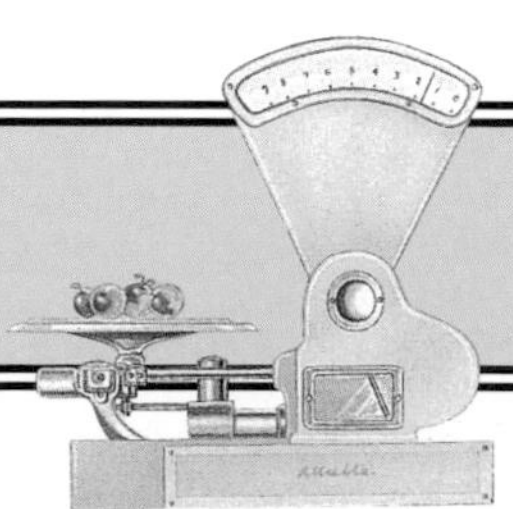

INDEX